Go Tell It

Go Tell It

and Other Poems

by

Sherwood Eliot Wirt

Beacon Hill Press of Kansas City
Kansas City, Missouri

Copyright, 1979
by Sherwood Eliot Wirt

No item nor part thereof may be reproduced in any form
without written permission from the author.

ISBN: 0-8341-0580-2

Printed in the United States of America

Acknowledgment is made to *Decision* magazine, Minneapolis,
for granting permission to use a number of the poems herein which
originally appeared in that publication during the many years
that the author served as its editor.

Dedication

To Virginia Caine Cooper
Filia sororis amantissima

Contents

11	Go Tell It
17	Visitation
18	Greatness
20	Cana
21	Lei Day
23	Open Up
25	Girl of San Sisto
28	Inscriptus
28	Leashed
29	Turnabout
30	Myrrh
31	John in Gethsemane
32	Palm Sunday
33	Solution
33	Witness
34	The Race
36	Kairos
37	Gone!
37	Psalm Nine
38	Fifth Season

39	Rope Trick
40	Rumblings
41	Immanuel
42	Easter Walk
45	Branch
46	Curtain Time
47	Win and Lose
48	Pre-Board Screening
50	White Stone
52	To John Knox
54	Back Pew
55	Silver Helmet
57	Two Men
57	Diapason
58	Fighting Animal
59	Silent Night
60	Jordan
61	Zoological Note
62	Early Christians
63	Interruption

Preface

It is particularly gratifying to write the preface for this volume, which brings together the poems I have written over a period of 28 years. It is an answer to aspiring poets who despair of ever having their work published; and an answer to publishers who are convinced that no market exists for Christian poetry.

The truth is that an enormous demand exists in North America for inspirational poetry that captures truth, carries an inner rhythm, exalts God, makes sense, and breathes the culture of the late 20th century. Some of the poems in this collection rhyme; most do not. That too is a reflection of the mood of the time.

Most of these poems appeared in the 1960s and 1970s in *Decision* magazine, but many were written earlier, and a few since I left the editorial chair of that publication.

I wish to thank Dr. J. Fred Parker, book editor of the Nazarene Publishing House, whose encouragement is responsible for this modest and rather shy venture into a glorious art form.

—S. E. W.

Go Tell It

Go
tell it on the mountain
that Jesus Christ is born.

A rather singular idea when you reflect on it
for who lives on the mountain?
    bighorned sheep marmots and edelweiss
    and woodpeckers in a toppled ponderosa
    untouched by Adam's sin.

If Christ is really born in our midst
    God with us
        Immanuel
        the Savior of the world
might we not better proclaim Him where people are
    where the human voice will carry
    in the ghettos suburbs trailer parks
    condominiums dormitories high-rises
    low-rents hospitals and prisons
    and *every Middlesex village and farm*

might we not better share the Christ child
   with the pushers
   and fender benders
   and politicians
   and heart patients
   and decent godless folk
who don't live on mountains?

Let's rewrite the song,
   forget the mountain.

Yet which mountain are we to forget?

Shall we forget Moriah
   on whose summit Abraham our father
   prepared to sacrifice a son
   to the will of God?
No. Go tell Moriah of another Son
   God's own Son, a Christmas Gift
   from the Father to us
   the one all-sufficient Sacrifice for sin.

Shall we forget Sinai
   where barefoot Moses took the Law?
No. Tell Sinai
   that men are saved not by Title II of the
     Senate bill
   or Section Eight of the Penal Code
     but by grace and truth in Christ Jesus.

Shall we forget Tabor
    where Barak and Deborah ran down
    upon the iron chariots of Sisera?
No. Tabor needs to hear
    of One who climbed its peak to be transfigured
        not the provocateur of war
        but the beloved Son of the Father.

Shall we forget Nebo
    from whose apex the Israelite viewed
    the land of promise?
No. Let Nebo know
    of a land fairer than Canaan
    untroubled by import-export quotas
    and long hot summers of despair
        where power runs down from the watershed
        and a man can build in peace.

Shall we forget Mount Zion
    where the Lord God roared and Israel trembled?
    Rather tell it on Jerusalem mountain
that the prophecy of Jeremiah has come to pass
        through the immeasurable love of a Nazarene
    in circumcision of the heart
        and in loaves
        and fishes
        and tribal dispensaries.

Shall we forget the Mount of Beatitudes
    where Jesus sat and opened His mouth and spoke
    as no man ever spake?
Shall we forget that unknown crest
    where a solitary Figure prayed all night
or the Mount called Olivet
    with its Gethsemane
    where Holiness drank the bitter cup
for us?
Shall we forget the green hill far away
shall we forget
shall we forget Calvary?

Oh, sing it again
tell it on the mountain
scale the snowy summits with a new story
raise up antenna towers on the crags and pinnacles
    for us in the land of walk and don't walk
so skipping children will know
    that when God delivered His people
        the mountains skipped
so youth clapping the beat will know
    that when God keeps His promise in that day
        the mountains will break into singing
        and the trees of the field will clap.

Tell the poor and heartsick and insecure
    that the Virgin Mary had a baby Boy
    that to us is born a Savior

>   Christ the Lord;
> and He shall redeem the whole creation
>   in that day when every knee shall bow
>   and mountains and all hills
> shall praise Him.

Mountains yes
Shasta   Cook   Whitney   Rainier   Kennedy
Washington Eisenhower
Pikes Peak and Chimney Rock
Denali and Fairweather, Skiddaw and Ben Lomond
Blue Mountains and Snowy
Lhotse and Annapurna, Everest and K2
Shiprock and Kilimanjaro
Fuji and Mauna Kea and Popocatepetl,
and all the high Alps and Andes—
they shall praise Him.

Go tell it on the mountain
that the Glory of the mountain is with us
    and the Glory of the valley is with us
that Jesus Christ is born.

Go tell it
Go tell it
how beautiful upon the mountain
are the feet of him that bringeth good tidings
    that death has died
    that Love is coming for His own

in a moment to be
    when those blessed
        feet shall stand
astride headlands and promontories of the earth
proclaiming glad tidings of great joy to all people
and men who know Him
    shall lift their eyes beyond the hills
to the Lord of peace
who shall publish His peace forever and forever.
Hallelujah!

Visitation

I knelt beside a lonely lake
    Where all was green and blue;
I asked the Lord to take my life
    And fashion it anew.
And as I knelt, a breath I felt
    Of glory in that place;
The Spirit of the Living God
    Came down in power and grace.

The wind soughed gently through the trees;
    No other sound was heard,
But as of yore Christ walked the shore
    And broke to me His Word;
And angel trumpets filled the air
    In praise to God the Son,
And all the pine trees clapped their hands
    At what the Lord had done.

Greatness

Do you see that old man lying there
in purple, on that box of solid gold?
Two days ago he was alive, if you can
call it that. An ulcerated groin
with maggots, tumors in his feet, spasms,
fevers, pain, intolerable itching. Oh,
he was great, he was. Herod the Great.
And just what did he do, this so-great one,
apart from executing kin by hundreds,
murdering his own wife and family,
conniving, torturing, betraying,
massacring the infant males of Bethlehem?
"Actually he was an excellent ruler." So
Enslin. But soon that stately, gleaming Temple—
white marble overlaid with gold and jewels—
was torched by Titus's legionaries. Taxes
dropped, but rose again. The Olympic Games
soon ceased. And Herod's pitch for fame—
glorifying his name with colonnades,
porticos, cloisters, aqueducts, harbors,
fortresses, amphitheaters, gymnasiums,
statues, monuments—all came to nothing;
they make the Mediterranean rubble. So it is,
said Jesus, with those who go the human

route to greatness. And Augustus quipped,
"I'd rather be a pig than Herod's son."
Now over here is something else to note:
a Jewish Child wound up in bandages
and lying in a trough where oxen feed.
OK. What else is new? Let's not stay here.
This smelly cave, these common peasant types,
with their weird accent from some dull
provincial place up north, are not the most
favorable environment for greatness—
certainly not the thing I had in mind.
But wait a moment. Remember that old man
dying of worms in all that panoply!
The Holy Book speaks somewhere does it not
of that which is the very least of all
becoming great? Look at this tiny Babe
and see if you can the Savior of the world
taking away the piled-up guilt of millions
and pouring out the love of God the Father
by His Spirit. You speak of greatness. What
if I show you music, literature, art
that is as magnificently beautiful
today as when it first was born in the soul
of a Christ-enthralled believer? What if I
show you a runaway convert, timid with hope,
on her way home for Christmas? I tell you
greatness is not what Herod thought it was.
Greatness is Jesus whom he sought to kill.

Cana

So this is what You mean, Lord
    from experience comes hope
    from faith comes fortitude
    from love comes completion
in Your joy. But what of all
those lost, unpatterned hours?
Were they not waste?
Or do they now
add filmy lace to whiteness
and poignancy to prayers
of gratitude? It's hard to say.
All I know is
earth is a lonely place
without Your Spirit's presence
and when I see Your hand
stitching these two hearts into a
design for eternity I take
new heart and say
Praise God! You did it, Lord.
You did a beautiful work.
All over Palestine that day
were men conducting weddings
but only one miracle.

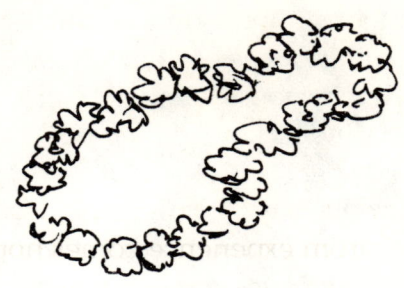

Lei Day

Your name is Yasuko
and you live among the green combers of sugar
in a white-painted house in Ewa
where today is May Day,
and because May Day is Lei Day in Hawaii
you are off to the kindergarten program
    with a picnic lunch
        and a lei.
It is a beautiful Saturday morning
a time for children and flowers
for gentle games and singing in the park.
You are not aware—
it has not broken into your purview
that May Day has become a signal,
the dead calling to the living
and a celebration of military hardware

as rocket wagons rumble on the cobblestones
    daubed with slogans of doublespeak
        paraded by goose-stepping mechanisms
      with windup keys in their backs.
You have not seen
Molotov cocktails hurled at the embassy wall
or hostages pushed out of upper windows
and falling to the pavement heavy with bullets.
No one has told you yet
that a few miles from where you live
are lying two thousand young men
just below the warm surface of ultramarine blue
in the quiet waters of the harbor
where they have lain near forty years.

Run along, Yasuko,
you will pick it all up soon enough
and tomorrow you will take your mother's hand
and go wherever it is you go on Sunday
but who will tell you the other part of life?
The part that is beyond flowers
    and distress signals
        and bombs and armament!
Who will lead you into the throne room of
      the Most High
    or seat you at the banquet table of the Messiah?

Open Up

I rolled a stone
in front of my heart
and hung out a sign
that said
      KEEP OUT
while I set about my life work
accumulating

snakes rats   roaches
      spiders   salamanders

and other specimens
of contemporary culture—
until God spoke
one morning in early spring
through brilliant sunshine,
saying,
"That stone has to go."

I asked, "Why?"

He said
"Because it is Easter
    and He has just left
      Joseph's tomb
    and is starting out
for yours."

*For the Black Monks of San Sisto
in Piacenza, Raphael painted a
picture for the high altar . . . truly
a work most excellent and rare.*
— Giorgio Vasari
(1511-74)

Girl of San Sisto

*(On viewing the Sistine Madonna
in Dresden, East Germany)*

Vasari said black monks of Piacenza
far to the north and out of culture's way
came seeking the young men of Perugia
for a church painting. Which they got, but when?
And where? And why on canvas, of all things?
There are no sketches left; no history
of lines and planes and masses, light and shade,
wine reds and violet grays and greens and blues
mixed by the hand of genius in between
a frantic round of more important tasks
(frescoes and tapestries, rooms of the Vatican);
no history, just silence. And a mother
with her Son, which the Italian monks
sold in due time to German Saxony
for cash.

But have you seen this work? And have you caught
the wonder of San Sisto's masterpiece?
Gazed into those dark eyes of holy faith
that look—or do they look? Or just look through
a world that never quite believed her tale?
Let the eyes pass. Here is a face quite young,
spangled with innocence from brow to chin;
here is a maid who ponders in her heart
the mystery of Christmas Eve, and Him
who gave her Child to lift the world from sin,
and knows the sparrow's fall, and made the breath
that billows out the veil that wraps her round
in loveliness and purity.

Beside her cheek there rests the Son of God,
wearing the grave visage of infancy;
about to speak, perhaps? No. Perhaps not.
"Mine hour is not yet come." Yet grace and truth,
authority and reconciling love,
are all enshrined in childlike mystery
right here. And a great voice beyond the sun
comes through the speakers of the universe,
invades the stereos and TV sets:
"Here is the One you waited for: Behold!"
Defuse the transmitters and ground the jets,
unhook the phones and jam the slot machines;
the Prince of Peace has visited the earth,
and shall He find true faith? What shall He find?

A world of potheads, sports, and burning saints?
"Herein is love, not that you have loved Me,
but I have loved you, and am come to save
that which is best, and which is rotten worst,
if you will come. I see a shadow rise
upon an ugly hill: I know that stony path.
If that is what you cost, I am prepared;
I bid you Merry Christmas."

In Dresden's Royal Gallery a guard
stands with his gun; he cocked it 20 years
ago, and still the *Sowjet* mans his post
amid the pallor of the DDR
and tells the people: "Either Red or dead."
One quiet room he keeps his distance from,
where hangs a painting of a sweet-faced girl
holding God's Son for heaven and earth to see,
and know, and glorify. He walks aloof
while drab-clothed pilgrims wander in and sit
and cry. Perhaps he heard it long ago—
*The Christmas Child will come again with eyes
a flame of fire, to judge the world, to sift—*
The "bourgeois fable" did not register. But soon
(how soon?) his piece will clatter to the floor
as adamantine glory fills the earth.
Praise God from whom the season's blessings flow;
Shalom, Madonna! *Addio,* black monks,
and thank you, Raphael.

Inscriptus

And did they pin a button
on Your swaddling clothes
and did it say One Way
or Have a Nice Forever?
Or did it read
This is Jesus
the King of the Jews?

Leashed

He tames the savage beast
    In our behavior
And binds us to himself,
    Our Lord and Savior.

Nor to himself alone
    But to each other—
"If you love Me," He said,
    "Love one another."

Turnabout

Say I was there
taking it in,
where would you put me?
Standing and weeping with
Mary
    Mary
        and John?
Sitting in the bleacher section
with the clowns
hurling insults at Holiness?
Kneeling by the upright
Waiting my turn at dice?
You're wrong.
I would have been streaking
  down the road,
robe aloft, elbows like pistons,
cutting toward a Roman culvert
and diving under it.
Which makes it all the more, you see,
a work of supernatural grace
for a faithful, saving Lord
to pull me out
and spin me round
and send me back.

Myrrh

To perfume His body
Magi brought myrrh to Jesus.
He didn't need it
He was already
the Fragrance of the universe.

To deaden the pain
soldiers mixed wine with myrrh.
He didn't need it
even as He bled
He was filled with the Spirit.

To wrap with the body
women brought myrrh with ointment.
He didn't need it
the tomb was an interlude.
God had made other plans.

John in Gethsemane

The grass is pleasant here
    rains have given the earth a chance to soften.
I wonder we have not come to Gethsemane
    more often.

We are worn out from the Temple crowds
    I can hardly stay awake.
I wish He would join us and get some rest
    for His own sake.

But ever since supper He has seemed strange—
    something on His mind—
I expect it will all work out tomorrow
    and we can unwind.

How drowsy it all seems this evening
    and the earth
        how kind.

Palm Sunday

Let's see
    one unbroken colt
    fresh-cut branches
    several dozen odd garments
    a pick-up crowd
and that ought to do it:
    Palm Sunday.
But suppose it backfires
    suppose the Triumphal Entry
    ends five days later
    on an execution post
    in a refuse heap
would you say God
could salvage our salvation
out of that?

Solution

There are people
    waiting
        waiting
           waiting
for man?
No.
Man has exhausted their patience.
What does man offer but broken plays
and unfinished puzzles?
They are waiting for God.
They are waiting for the angel
to roll away
the stone.

Witness

Cast me, Lord,
as a bell
    of molten bronze
pitched to the ear of man.
Cool me a bit
harden me
    and let me ring.

The Race

It was late afternoon on the last day
when I saw two men leap out of their starting blocks
and stride down the track in opposite directions
and I thought
"Look, this is not according to AAU guidelines"
so I jogged alongside one
as he ran out into the street and dug his spikes
into the asphalt
and I said, "What? Why? Where? Have you
           considered?"
And he laughed
as he loped through a red light.
"Of course I have considered," said he.
"I want to see everything.
I want life and I want to live
quaff the goblet and drain the dregs
flex the muscles and pump the legs
you'll catch me at Indy for the five hundred
Lauderdale for spring break
Edinburgh for the festival
Cannes and Venice and San Francisco for the flicks
I'll be drawing for twenty-one at Macau
and taking in Moscow for the games
and wherever there's my kind of music
count me in.

None of it means anything," he said
"but I'm going
and I don't mean anything either."
I looked around for the second runner.
He was cutting straight across country when I found him
and the sky was overcast and he was carrying
a torch. "Where to?" I asked.
"Heaven," he said.
"Do you mean anything?" I asked
struggling to keep up.
"I mean Christ crucified and risen," was his answer
and a burning was in his eye
as he flung the blazing torch
to me.
And the thunder clapped as he raced up a hill.
"Hurry," he said, "there is still time—
a time and times and half a time
and multitudes in the valley of decision
crying for hope."
I looked and he was gone
and the trail he had been following
flickered red with blood.

Kairos

The evening, the evening,
straw in the cave and drowsy animals in the dark
a woman's cry
and stardom set afire with unearthly music:
This was Christmas Eve.

The afternoon, the afternoon,
three poles of men and thick clouds racing past
and nails and blood
and dice and spears, and sin and tears
    as Someone died
for me:
This was Good Friday.

The morning, the morning,
the laughter of old olive trees at human consternation
as Jesus, Victor Jesus, put the atoms and the whole
world back together,
and turned the corner of history and of life itself:
This was Easter.

The noontime, the noontime,
the Word was preached and I was saved
and glory spilled about;
the angels sang of newborn life and peace on earth:
And it was Christmas Eve again.

Gone!

The rock
the Roman lock
what is there to it?
How did He do it?

They tell me He is risen
out of death's prison
but how can that be?
What did they see?

O terror of that daybreak hour
O rapture of the Savior's power
O Life that broke but did not bend
O grave that burst from end to end!

Psalm Nine

Lord, if I dig a pit for others
let me fall into it;
but if I dig it for myself,
give me sense enough to walk around.

© *Christian Century,* 1954

Fifth Season

Good for man is the movement of the seasons
the slow pulse of nature:
    spring in fresh ecstasy
    summer warming the earth
    autumn in waning glory
    and winter: bare, white, inspiriting.

How could one of these be called best?
Who chooses among jewels
in the crown of the King?

My heart speaks to me of another season
a fifth season that greets all seasons
God's own time
    which He made
        which He honors
            which He loves:
My heart speaks of the season of prayer.

Rope Trick

He was, he said, just about at the end
of his tether
when it happened.
While his God watched
someone said something at lunch
about Jesus
and he decided to take one more weekend
to give his soul a chance
before he coiled the tether into a loop.
That Sunday evening he wandered
                into a church.
Now,
while his God watches
he is throwing a rope to his neighbor
his body has found peace and likes him
his soul loves the Lord
he is a walking arrangement of the
                "Hallelujah Chorus"
no one really understands but the angels
    and they are busy with the music.

Rumblings

Rhythm . . .
His rhythm . . .
I see it in the falling of the leaves
the turning of the salmon toward fresh water
the swinging of the planets about the sun
    youth and age
      birth and death
      shadow and sunrise.
I hear it in the surge of tide and the dropping
    of cones
the majesty of the twenty-seventh psalm
the hidden cadences of the body
    breathing
        beating
            cleansing.
All these speak in rhythm
of God.

O that my mind would halt its
    uneven

        z i g z a g

and listen to the rhythm of the earth
as it speaks
of God.

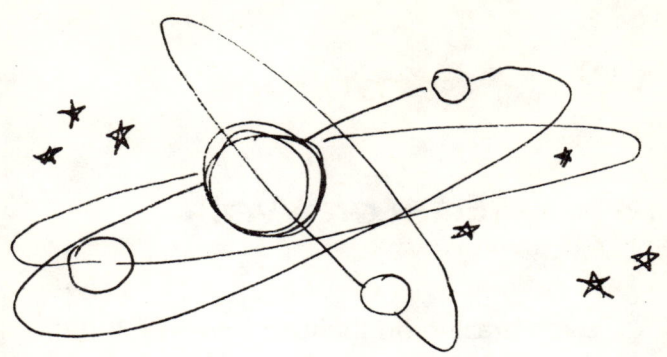

Immanuel

You brought no souvenirs
no holy packages
from the glory zones,
only Yourself.
You passed through no heat
in Your descent to Bethlehem,
but we took care of it
in our own way.
Your aerie
up there in the bell tower
was beyond our reach
so we burned it down.
Well, that's life.
What a mess.
We're glad You brought us
something better.

Easter Walk

Lamb grazing on the warm green hillside
I watch you frisking white and lovable
but let me ask you something:
What do you know about fabric shortages
or the rising demand for wool?
It's some world you've come to, little one.
I wouldn't give much for your future.
Save for the blood of the Lamb
I wouldn't give much for ours either.

This is the rueful generation
that painted itself into a corner.
Imagine no trips to the lake at Easter!
These are the sidewalk people
of Toowoomba and Ealing and West Fargo
who want to know who's in charge here,
while at Louie's and Harry's and Lucky's
they mutter over Reuben sandwiches
about the drop in the resort trade
and troubles in truck parts
and Christmas tree lights.

What can be done for these people?
Who can save them?

Climbing the hill to the crest
I look over wild distant deserts
and catch a glimpse of a solitary figure—
young, thin, dressed in skins, shouting:
You built a tower
 without counting the cost.
You sowed the wind
and reaped the whirlwind.
You put flags on the moon
and junked cars on the outskirts.
You ate from the tree of knowledge
and blew your minds.
You prefabbed your temples
and stayed in your sins.
You had a ball
and the ball was the earth.
   O generation of vipers
              repent
              repent
              repent!

And I watch as he kneels in prayer.
But now he stands erect, head high
and points to One coming: "At last He is here.

Come and see! Behold the Lamb of God
who takes away the sin of the world."
And I see crowds flocking to the desert
and I think we're not down the tube
yet.
There is hope.

Walking to the other side of the hill
I see a tomb knocked awry
and soldiers lying about as if dead
and in the sky flashes of lightning
and seven torches of fire
with voices and peals of thunder
and harpists playing on their strings.
I see angels gathered about a throne
and hear them singing:
> Worthy is the Lamb that was slain.
> The kingdom of the world
> has become the Kingdom of our Lord
> and of His Christ
> and He shall reign for ever and ever.

All this on an Easter afternoon
while the new lambs grazed and frolicked
on the warm green hillside
and the old world turned the key
on an empty tank.

Branch

God gave me grapes great
clusters of them
then He took them away.
Naturally I sulked.
"It hardly pays to be a branch,"
    I muttered;
and wouldn't you know it, my next grapes
    were bitter.
So God said, "You can keep them
I can't use them";
and they went to the birds.

Pruning time,
and the sweetness of the Lord came
pouring in from the Vine
and I said,
"Father I'm a pretty sorry branch,
but take me—I'm all yours."
He said, "Son,
    give me grapes."

Curtain Time

Hammer hammer hammer
   stadium crew
six hours to go
   so much to do.
Fresh clean lumber
   ten-penny nails
steps to Jesus
   with handrails
steps to the green turf
   sacred sod
home of the Giants
   home of God.
Thousands coming
   to hear the man
offering Jesus
   God's great plan.
Walk ye the way
   walk ye the walk
Christ wants action
   not just talk.
Test those risers
   make them hold.

    I have a son
        Twenty years old
    he needs help
        and he just might
    walk these steps
        to heaven tonight.

Win and Lose

Not for the avenues of shade and sun
which I have walked, and shall walk by His leave;
nor for the dubious joy of weeping birth,
the struggle to mature, the fight for life,
the tiny victories and vast defeats,
the teaspoon-fillings of all human love,
the aching loss of separated hearts:
not for these reasons do I love the Lord.

I love the Lord because of who He is—
for this: I cannot help my loving Him
who loosens my thick tongue so I can pray,
and prays through me, and answers His own prayer;
who takes my life, redeems what I call loss,
then takes my best and nails it to the cross.

Pre-Board Screening

Sitting in the pew
listening to the preacher
I heard him describe in elegant
turn of phrase
the Valley of Contentment.
He said planes left every hour.
Immediately I cancelled all my appointments
to head for that valley
my ticket being simply
the assurance of the Holy Spirit
that I was already in Christ.
During the choral benediction I
slipped out
    grabbed a taxi
        made for the airport

sans luggage
    sans insurance
but full of confidence and hope.
Humming I sauntered toward the gate
when the inspector stopped me.
"This way, sir." "Why?" "Security check."
I walked the electronic plank
a high tone sounded, lights flashed.
"Right over here." "Now what?" "Sorry.
Your reading on the love dial is
below our minimums." He handed me a tray.
I felt in all the pockets of my soul
and found a dozen hard and bitter things
I didn't know were there. Shamefacedly
I laid them on the tray.
"Walk through again." Chastened
I did as I was told
and sensed a marvelous new peace.
"When does the flight leave?" I inquired.
He grinned. "You're there already."

Then came an ectoplasmic blur.

               Softly the organ
invaded my reverie. I looked up
and heard the preacher
announce the closing hymn.

*To him that overcometh will I
give . . . a white stone, and in the
stone a new name written, which
no man knoweth saving he that
receiveth it.* —Rev. 2:17

White Stone

Tiger crouching by the TV set
who took away your forest?
Who sneaked off with the whole green dazzling world
and left you but a flickering image of it?
Where did they hide the acorns
   the buckeyes, the bullfrogs
      the squirrel guns
         the nights on pine needles
            the hardtack and cheese
               the molasses candy pulls
                  the expeditions to Lost Lake
                     and the spelunking at Wildcat Caves?
Our heart goes out to you, Tiger,
even though you don't hear us
because you are watching the antihero
   push his grandmother
      down the stairs
         in her wheelchair.
This age of sound has deafened you.
The nuclear chain reaction was too much
for your shell baby ears

and so today you crouch
crippled, caged,
your schoolbooks unheeded,
your mind uneasily aware that the universe now belongs
to the computers.
All you really want is the forest that was
that is now an attractive development
    with lots going fast
and nothing is left but the Man from Planet X
beating up somebody
and ripping off the fuzz
until the tired tube winks out.

Listen, Tiger, I have news for you.
You don't have to stay eyeballed to that screen.
God has a stone
for your long-neglected rock collection,
a white stone
and on it a name inscribed that only you can decipher
but with that stone, the world is yours.
It's a world to win, Tiger,
a thrilling world, a glorious world,
a world of champions and more than champions,
of forests and summits and radiant wonder
    and hearts that look to you with a quick smile
        and brave men and clean girls
           and comradeship
               and adventure the human race
                    thought lost forever.

It's there, Tiger, if you want it,
if you pick up that Book and read it.
Don't bother to flick off the set—let it go;
if you keep reading you'll get your hearing back
and you'll be deaf to everything
but the voice of the One who made you.

I see you stirring; the man is talking about corn chips.
God bless you, Tiger, you're hungry.
You wonder what's in the . . .

Take, eat. This is My Body, which is broken for you.

To John Knox

> Gentler spirits have lived
> in Christendom,
> more gracious messengers preached
> the Word of Christ
> without a-dinging the pulpit,
> but God knew what He was doing
> when He chose you
> to build His church.

He knew the temptations to compromise
the dulcet voice pleading in tears
the soft hand of scheming sovereignty.
You were as keen as steel,
as deaf as ice:
God's man
for God's work
in God's time.

© *Christianity Today*, 1972

Back Pew

Explain it in the common tongue,
    In phrases clearly understood,
Just how it was for me He hung,
    For me was shed this kingly Blood.

For only vaguely do I sense
    Your meaning, Reverend, and it's late,
And really I mean no offense—
    But speak up, man! Communicate!

I want to know how I can trust
    A joiner on a Roman rack
To make eternal life from dust
    And get this sin load off my back.

So keep to basics if you can—
    This heart's an empty void to fill;
And if you can't . . .
      Lord! . . .
          help this man!
And lead me to someone who will.

*He put . . . an helmet of
salvation upon his head.*
  —Isa. 59:17

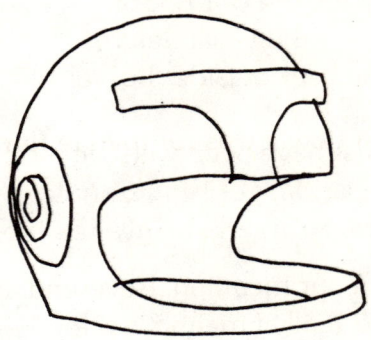

Silver Helmet

I snapped the chronometer to "hold"
and stepped out of my time capsule.
There he was, standing at the crest of the rise
　　feet spread
　　　　one arm akimbo
　　　　　　the other shading his face
as he surveyed the road ahead.
He lifted his hand in greeting and I followed his eye.
"Expecting to meet someone?"
"Yes," he said.

"Well, now," I went on, "I think I've seen you
                    somewhere,
         at Krakatoa
              or at the time of the Lisbon earthquake
                   or the fire of London
                        or the black death
or was it one year outside the walls of Jerusalem?"
He shook his head.
"Then it must have been with Tiglath-Pileser in Samaria
     or at the landing of King Canute
          or when Tamerlane invaded the steppes."
"No," he said.
"Then was it at Ai? Carthage? Toledo? Calcutta?
Auschwitz or Hiroshima?"
"At none of these," he said, looking straight ahead.
"Are you headed somewhere?" I asked.
"I shall walk this road," he said,
"and watch for the return of my Friend."
"Will He come?"
"Yes," he said, "He will come."
I glanced at the capsule with its idling fuel system.
"If you had a choice," I asked,
"would you have chosen a year
     with less prospect of misery and hatred
          more promise of glory?"
"I am this year," he said. "There is no other."
He clapped on a silver crash helmet.
"Take heart," he said. "God lives. Good cheer."
And he started down the road.

Two Men

There were two men in the city
the one rich, the other poor
and the Spirit rested on them both
as they went up to the temple
to pray.
They prayed for each other.
The one who was rich
became poor in spirit
and the one who was poor
became rich in love
and God filled the temple
      with incense.

Diapason

Come Holy Spirit
play upon the organ of my heart
woo me gently
with melodies of Your
salvation then
           pull out all the stops.

Fighting Animal

All day long he played cowboys
Indians
soldiers
broken death in his holster
blunt shafts in his quiver:
Solidly embattled he
closed with the universe and
    gave no quarter
for who can give quarter to
bad guys?

Yet that night
cheeks scrubbed, teeth gleaming,
    eyes sandy
arms around the neck—
a sigh came, and a whisper:
"Mommy
I don't want to go to war."

And her heart stood still
as she prayed.

Silent Night

Hush!
No squeaking among you bats
mice stop that gnawing
rats keep away from the hay
cat cease your yowling feed those kittens
donkeys don't you dare hee-haw
oxen go on ruminating
but see you do it noiselessly
we want no lowing cattle here
no bleating goats
dogs put an end to that barking
roosters back on your perches.
Quiet
I say, QUIET, universe
flag down those comets
muffle those meteors
the King of kings is slumbering.

Jordan

A silver trickle
bifurcates the land
and laves the world
with hope.
Here priests of God
cross over
into the Promise
with the sacred ark.
A four-star leper
wades ashore:
"God in Israel!
I'm clean!"
A desert rat
standing knee-deep
in the shallows
cries out, "Repent!
Come wash!"
A voice breaks out
of Heaven: "You
are My Son, the Beloved."
And we?

We camp on shore
and play at war
    east bank
    west bank
    your tank
    my tank
while that silver trickle
gently laves the world
with hope.

Zoological Note

I sent Christmas greetings to our pet
and on the card I wrote
"Will you be ready
      ready for His advent?"
but I needn't have bothered
for when He came
it was the animals that took Him in,
      not we.

Early Christians

Midsummer dawns early
in Bithynia
where they joined hands
on an ancient hilltop
    so I read the Roman Pliny
to sing their hymns to Christ
as God
to share their love
and pray.
Beautiful people
early Christians.
Lord, make me one
early to sing of Jesus
early to reach out in love
to my brother and sister
early to the Cross
    and the empty tomb.

Interruption

To think that
I might not even
finish this poem
before the Lord comes
and all the—
sorry!
Must go.